Unleashing the Gift

Donald Douglas

Unleashing the Gift

www.RATHSIPUBLISHING.COM

Copyright @ 2012 by Donald Douglas

ISBN 978-1-936937-30-1

Foreword

Sometimes there is no compulsion to write; no hankering desire, or no will. Other times, there is a small still voice that whispers, 'you have a story to tell'. Thank God Author Donald Douglas listened to that small still voice and responded with this compelling novel, "Unleashing the Gift". If you have ever wondered what your divine purpose was or why you have been blessed in the way that you have, wonder no more! This book not only establishes Donald Douglas as a divinely gifted writer but reestablishes his divine gifts as a man of God. You will be challenged and encouraged after reading Mr. Douglas' prolific work, "Unleashing the Gift!"

Deidra D. S. Green,

Best Selling Author of "Closet Issues","Epiphanies While Driving" and "Here Comes Katrina".

Dedication

I want to dedicate this book to everyone who reads it and whose gifts are going to be unleashed after reading this book.

Preface

It was prophesied to me almost 20 years ago that I would write a book. At the time those words were spoken to me, about me, I immediately began to come up with all the reasons why I wouldn't or couldn't write a book. I was not a writer, and if I did sit down to actually 'write a book', what would I say? So I took what was spoken to me and tucked it away. From time to time, I would be reminded of those words spoken to me. Again, I would think of why I couldn't, wouldn't, or shouldn't write a book. I convinced myself that my gifts were in other areas and would again, tuck the prophesy away, never really giving it much thought.

Fast forward almost 20 years. Up until recently, I had given little thought to the words that were spoken to me oh so many years ago. It was just something in the back of my mind, not even on the back burner. And then I heard the words again. Although the words were spoken from a different person, something about what was said begin to register in my spirit and the originally prophesy was brought back to my remembrance. For the first time, I didn't immediately negate the words that were spoken. I actually began to think about the prospects of actually writing a book! This time when all the reasons why I shouldn't, wouldn't or couldn't came up, instead of allowing them to affect my thoughts, I began to combat the negativity with all the reasons why I could, should and would write a book.

Immediately upon my acceptance of the possibilities of

authorship, I was gifted with the idea for and the direction of the book, and "Unleashing the Gift!" was born.

I pray the words and spirit poured out onto these pages touches you in such a way that the should not's, would not's, and could not's in your life are replaced with the shoulds, coulds and woulds, and will!

Acknowledgements

"Do not neglect the gift which is in you, [that special inward endowment] which was directly imparted to you [by the Holy Spirit] by prophetic utterance when the elders laid their hands upon you [at your ordination]". <u>1 Timothy 4: 14</u>

I want to give all praise to my daddy, Father God, for depositing the things mentioned in this book inside of me. He is the author and finisher of my faith and if it had not been for Him this would not be possible. Also I want to acknowledge and thank my beautiful wife and three lovely children for believing in me and allowing me to take time to finish such an awesome task. Finally, I want to thank my mentor who pushed me and God gave her the desire to help birth this book, my best friend, Deidra Green. God used her to unleash the rivers of living water during a time when I thought there were none. Thank you sis.

What is a Gift?

From as far back as I can remember, I have always enjoyed receiving gifts; whether it was a secret valentine shared between classmates, a birthday present after the candles on the cake had been blown out, or those gifts found under the tree after Santa had made his Christmas eve visit, it was something about receiving a present that said to me someone was thinking of me... someone cared enough about me to give me something special.

And that is what a gift really is... something special given willingly without any expectation of payment or something in return. A gift is something that is given voluntarily as a kind gesture, in honor of a special occasion, or as a gesture of assistance.

Just thinking about those times when I have been the recipient of a gift, regardless of the circumstances, always makes me smile. Whether it was something small and personal or something extravagant and over the top, my happiness was most often the end result.

As I became older and matured, I began to understand the pleasure involved in not just the receiving of a gift but the giving of a gift. It was exciting to think about the person, the reason the gift was being selected, taking the time to pick out just the right gift that would show that person how I felt about them. Then, there were those anxious moments of waiting until they opened the gift. Would they like it? Did I make the right choice? Was there something else better I could have chosen? But then I would be relieved because their expression would let me know I had picked just the right gift for the right person at the right time. To see the eyes of a friend or family member light up when they opened a present I had selected especially for them, made me smile (as if I was the one receiving instead of giving).

That is how gifts in the natural make us feel; like someone cares, like we are special, like we matter. Gifts help us to earmark special occasions, highlight accomplishments, express our feelings and affections, and inform or remind the receiver of the gift, how we truly feel about him or her.

Unfortunately, there are those times, though, when the gifts we receive do not make us happy. And although we appreciate the gesture extended by the other individual, something about the gift is displeasing. That can be a very difficult moment for both the receiver and the giver. The giver is expecting the receiver to like the gift, appreciate the gift, and be thankful for the gift. The receiver on the other hand is trying not to show their true feelings on their face at the displeasure in the gift. The receiver tries to smile and feigns a well meaning 'thank you' and hopes against all hope the giver doesn't pick up on the fact that the gift was not what the receiver desired, wanted or expected. The receiver may have been appreciative of the gesture, but the gift itself fell flat.

I too have found myself in such a compromising and uncomfortable position. I am sure the giver meant well, but the gift was not something (a) I would have picked for myself, (b) something I desired, or (c) something I would have wanted anyone to pick for me! The truth of the matter is, upon receipt of the gift, I questioned whether or not that person really knew me, knew my taste, or even knew what would remotely make me happy. Of course, I abided by all the rules of etiquette, put a huge smile on my face, and said "thank you so much!" ... and then I prayed they would not discern the displeasure on my face.

Anytime something like this would happen, and I hate to admit it but it has happened to me on more than one occasion, it reminded me of those times when I was a child, making my wish list for Santa because I had been such a good boy that year. I would scour the toy sections of the major department store catalogues, comb through all the available selections, look for the toys that stood out to me and that I secretly wanted, and neatly make a list (in rank order file from most desirable to lesser desirable... but still desired none the less), written in perfect penmanship so Santa would have no question as to the Christmas gift I wanted the most. I would make sure the letter to Santa was mailed in plenty of time so there would be no question that he would know exactly what I wanted. Then as Christmas Eve approached, the excitement would grow as I waited for that very moment when I would open the gift of my desire. Christmas Eve would always be a difficult night to get through; the hours would move so slowly.

But get through it I would and on Christmas morning, before anyone would have to come in and wake me up, I would be up and ready to go to the tree and get my gift!

Without reservation I would tear open the Christmas wrapping paper, sometimes overlooking toys and gifts that may have been lower on my priority list, looking for that one special gift! And then it would happen... I would have gotten to the last gift with my name on it only to find that the gift I most desired was not there! What happened? Did Santa not get the list in time? Sure the other gifts were great, but where was the one I really, really, wanted? Was I not good enough that year to get the gift my heart desired? What could have possibly gone wrong?

And of course, once again I would have to be grateful for the gifts I had received... I mean they were on the list too, and I wanted them as well, but they were not THE gift! I would be reminded of how blessed I was to have received such wonderful gifts and I knew I was more fortunate than most. But in the back of my mind, there was some level of disappointment in not receiving the gift of my desire.

As I began to think about the idea of giving and receiving of gifts, I began to think about God; the gifts He bestows, and those who receive the gifts.

"Now there are distinctive varieties and distributions of endowments (gifts, extraordinary powers distinguishing certain Christians, due to the power of divine grace operating in their souls by the Holy Spirit) and they vary, but the [Holy] Spirit remains the same." 1 Corinthians 12: 4

"Every good gift and every perfect (free, large, full) gift is from above; it comes down from the Father of all [that gives] light, in [the shining of] Whom there can be no variation [rising or setting] or shadow cast by His turning [as in an eclipse]." James 1: 17

God is a bestower of gifts. His gifts are extraordinary and His bestowing of the gifts is free! I truly believe that because of the omnipotence of the Creator, he knows the gifts he will bestow to whom, from the very beginning... even before the foundation of man was laid. Can you imagine the thought, deliberation, and consideration that comes with such a gift... a gift determined for you even before your birth?

That kind of thoughtfulness and consideration may be hard to comprehend but it goes without saying, this is a gift that a great deal of thought has gone into. Because God knows each of us better than we know ourselves, the gift or gifts he bestows upon us are perfect gifts! Yes, there are variations in the gift according to the person, but the thought, consideration, and planning behind each gift He gives is the same.

Now I am sure you are wondering what Santa Claus and God have to do with each other. Well, please indulge me for just a moment. I know the notion of Santa bearing gifts may be trivial for some, but consider this. Think back on when you did believe in Santa Claus; when you believed he could deliver gifts around the world to every child in one night! Remember when you believed that you're being good or bad directly related to whether you received a desired gift or a lump of coal. Think back to when you sat on Santa's knee in the local mall and told him what you really wanted for Christmas, and he delivered as promised. Think about when, even if you didn't make a list of the gifts you wanted, somehow Santa knew just what to get you! You would wake up Christmas morning to find that you had been given wonderful gifts that would give you a great deal of enjoyment for a time, and fond memories that would last a lifetime.

There are a few commonalities between Santa Claus and God. First, both give gifts… I think we can all agree to that. Secondly, the gifts they give truly come without attachments. Think about it. Even when you misbehaved as a child, even if your behavior was atrocious on Christmas Eve, there was still a gift for you under the tree on Christmas morning. In other words, although good behavior was encouraged, your receiving of a gift was truly not contingent upon how you behaved. Santa gave you that gift without condition… so does God. Another thing Santa and God have in common is that they sometimes give you a gift you haven't asked for but it is a gift nonetheless. You may not always regard it as the most desired gift or the best gift, but they (Santa or God) thought enough of you to give you a gift. Now, if you are honest with yourself, the gift you may not have desired may have provided you with the greatest level of entertainment or pleasure, and you found yourself at a later time, much more appreciative of that gift. Think about those times when you made a special request for a gift, whether on Santa's knee or in prayer to the

Creator, you asked for a gift and received it. Lastly, consider the fact that both Santa and God give gifts without expectation of receiving a gift in return. Sure, we left cookies and milk for Santa as a thank you for bringing us gifts. But is that the same as returning a gift to him? Consider this, even if you didn't leave cookies and milk, that following Christmas you would have gifts once again. Of course we thank God for the gifts he has bestowed upon us, if we first recognize them as gifts, but is that the same as giving Him a gift in return?

Hopefully you have noticed that I have referenced the gifts given by Santa or God as gifts and not presents. Of course these terms are often used interchangeably, but I intentionally did not use the term present. Why you ask? Because I want you to consider present in a different way; not present as in the synonym for gift but present as it relates to time.

Okay, take a moment and consider what I have just said... present as it relates to time. When you look up the word present in the dictionary, there are two definitions that are offered. One is a present, such as receiving of a gift and the other definition is 'the period of time now occurring'. In other words a present is a right now occurrence; not for some time in the future or only relatable in past tense. Present means right now!

When I consider how profound this concept is, I can't help but meditate on the omnipotence of God. The gifts that He so generously bestows upon each of us are relevant to our present day. The gift that God gives each one of us is a right now gift. The present He gives does not have an expiration date nor does it go out of style or become historical or unusable. Neither is the present He bestows a gift that is only usable for future reference, meaning it would not be relevant for present times. The gifts God gives are immediately relevant! They are a right now gift! What is even more miraculous about the presents God bestows is that they are always present! Don't miss this point. The gifts God bestows are always present. In other words, they are never out of season, out of step, or irrelevant. The gift remains a present. The gift evolves as we evolve and mature. The presents God gives are pansophic!

If you consider the present that God has so freely given you, the thought, consideration, love and care He took to make sure the gift you received was exactly right for you, then you will no longer question and wonder what a gift is.

Points to Consider...

Now that you have read the first chapter, here are some points to consider:

- ☐ **What were my prior thoughts about gifts and presents?**

- ☐ **What is my gift?**

- ☐ **What does the gift or gifts I have been given, mean in my life?**

- ☐ **Your thoughts...**

_____

_____

_____

_____

_____

_____

_____

_____

_____

_____

_____

_____

_____

_____

_____

_____

_____

_____

_____

_____

_____

_____

_____

Why is My Gift Not Working for Me?

Now that we know what a gift is and the timeliness of the gift from God, the next area to address is "Why isn't my gift working for me?

There are a number of reasons why your giftedness may not be fully operationalized; why you may feel your gift is not working for you. For each individual, the reasons may be different; however, there are some overriding issues that bear discussion as they serve to impact a number of individuals and inhibit giftedness.

One of the greatest inhibitors when it comes to operationalizing the gifts God has given can be the environment we grew up in. Whether we came from a broken home, a dysfunctional home or had an emotionally, psychologically or physically deprived upbringing, our environment can play a significant role in whether the gifts we have been given work for us. Let me give you a personal example. I have always been able to sing. From as far back as I can remember, I could sing. I was given the gift of son. As an adult, I can recall something my mother said: "Had I known he was going to be as gifted in this way, I would have invested in him a little bit more..."

The scripture, "train a child in the way he should go and when he gets older, he will not depart from it" (Proverbs 22:6) is one frequently quoted. Let's take a closer look at that scripture.

The word train in this context means educate or initiate. The way he should go refers to the child's natural inclination, what the child is good at, especially fitted for or the path especially belonging to. The ideal situation would be for a parent to "train a child in the way he or she should go"; however, for many of us, that training never took place. The reasons are numerous as to why, but as the old adage goes, there is really no use in crying over spilled milk.

Even if we were not given the proper support nor training as a child, does that make it okay to not actualize the gifts we've been given? Again, one of the best ways I know to make this point clear is to use a personal example. For any number of reasons and for the longest time, I didn't actualize the gifts I had received. Sure, I sang; I was good at singing… it came easy. But did I maximize the singing potential I was given? The answer to that is a definitive 'no'. For one, I took for granted that I would always be able to sing. I figured once I was in receipt of the gift, it was mine… Secondly, because I did not receive all the support in maturing and expanding my gift, I was lackadaisical about my gift. I didn't pursue it with vigor. The fact that without much effort, I could make my gift work for me and make room for me, I languished in my giftedness.

What I didn't do was make manifest the other gifts I was given. I made excuses for my gift and said that my gift wasn't working for me. In all actuality, I didn't work my gift! I didn't use the other talents and gifts I was given. It would have been easy for me to blame my environment, a lack of opportunity, a lack of self esteem, fear and any number of things, and I did for a very long time. So when I talk about why my gift didn't work for me, it is not just something I heard, it is something I have lived.

When it comes to environment, there is another component that needs to be considered. Of course the environments we grew up in can significantly impact the manifestation of our gifts. But equally as important is the current environment that we are in! Our current environment can support our gift and the growth of our gift or it can deter and inhibit our gift. We must be in a place where our gift can relate; where our gifts can work. Think about it. When you get in the right environment, your gift surges; it's like a baby kicking in the womb waiting to be birthed. An environment that is conducive to the full expression of our giftedness is what is required for our gift to truly work on our behalf for the edification of God.

Another reason why our gifts are not working for us is because of intimidation. That's right, intimidation. 'He preaches better than I do'; 'she is more learned than I am'; 'her faith is stronger than mine'; 'his ability to discern is keener than my own'. These are the negative messages that play in our heads. They do not emanate from an external source. This is not something someone else has said to us. This is our own personal negative self talk that we give voice to. The intimidation we may feel does not come from another person. It comes from within. The voice we often attribute to Satan or the devil is really us. We speak negativity into our own thoughts thus limiting and constraining our gifts. We see how others' gifts are being made manifest and are being operationalized and we become intimidated by what we perceive as the success or the giftedness of others.

If we are not careful with the spirit of intimidation, we can find ourselves not just limiting the use of our gifts but also becoming envious or jealous of the how other people's gifts are moving. God speaks very clearly about the power of having a jealous or envious spirit:

"For while there is jealousy and strife among you, are you not of the flesh and behaving only in a human way?" 1 Corinthians 3:3

"Surely resentment destroys the fool, and jealousy kills the simple." Job 5:2

When we allow feelings of intimidation to manifest into jealousy, we fail to allow our gifts to do what they have been designed to do. More than that, we discount the work that has been done by the other person who has intimidated us in the first place. Do we know how hard they may have prayed for their gifts to be unleashed? Do we know if they have fasted regarding their gifts? Do we know what struggles they may have had in getting their gifts to move? Do we have any idea what negative factors may have affected them; barriers they had to break through in order for their gift to become operationalized?

The other part of the intimidation factor is the work. Yes, God has given us these gifts. But there is work that must be done. Our gifts don't simply unleash themselves... it doesn't work that way. You are right! There are a number of people who can do what you do, who may have the same or a similar gift to what you have. That's why it is so important to put the work in. We have to sharpen our gifts. The focus is all wrong when intimidation becomes our focus and the limiter of our gifts. Take the focus off the other person and place the focus squarely where it belongs... with you!

Another factor that can prevent our gifts from working for us is poor self esteem. Self esteem is defined as an individuals' overall appraisal or evaluation of him or herself.

Self esteem includes beliefs and emotions that create one's self perception. This factor ties hand in hand with that of intimidation. Think about it... When we are not confident in who God called us to be; when we are not confident in our own abilities, we then look at the life and gifts of other people and our lack of self esteem causes the feeling of intimidation to reside within us.

How many of us routinely take self inventory? Are we honest with ourselves about our areas of strength and areas that may need improvement? What happens with a person who lacks self confidence is that they are unable to see the strengths and positives about themselves. Again, negative self talk and self doubt becomes a permanent partner in the thinking process and the only focus is on the limitations or areas of a persons' life that need to be improved. That is not... let me repeat... that is not an HONEST, OPEN, self evaluation. If you are operating with poor self esteem, your perception is deprived. Your ability to see yourself as a whole person instead of just your flaws is nonexistent.

That is why it is so very important to go back to God and His word when issues of poor self esteem plague our lives. God doesn't make mistakes! What He has put His hands to and what He has designed is not substandard.

"I will praise you; for I am fearfully and wonderfully made: marvelous are your works; and that my soul knows right well." Psalms 139:14.

Do you know this to be true? Do you believe what God says about you? Do you understand that you are wonderfully made by the hands of the Creator? Knowing this helps to assuage self doubt and poor self esteem. When you think about it, if you don't believe God did a good job with you, what are you really saying about Him? What do you really think of yourself?

One of the issues I struggled with, one of my personal gift inhibitors was complacency. I had gotten comfortable with where I was in my giftedness. Complacency is the feeling of being satisfied with yourself, where you are; unconcerned; content to a fault; not feeling compelled to move outside of your comfort zone; unawareness, even when controversy, danger or trouble lie ahead. I had gotten comfortable in my gift; right where it was; not feeling the need to sharpen my gift, to improve it in any way. "God gave it so me so that's enough," was my mantra. But I was unaware of the dangers that lie ahead for my gift. Let's talk about the realities concerning gifts and talents.

13 *"Therefore stay alert, because you do not know the day or the hour. 14 For it is like a man going on a journey, who summoned his slaves and entrusted his property to them. 15 To one he gave five talents, to another two, and to another one, each according to his ability. Then he went on his journey. 16 The one who had received five talents went off right away and put his money to work and gained five more. 17 In the same way, the one who had two gained two more. 18 But the one who had received one talent went out and dug a hole in the ground and hid his master's money in it. 19 After a long time, the master of those slaves came and settled his accounts with them. 20 The one who had received the five talents came and brought five more, saying, 'Sir, you entrusted me with five talents. See, I have gained five more.' 21 His master answered, 'Well done, good and faithful slave! You have been faithful in a few things. I will put you in charge of many things. Enter into the joy of your master.'*

22 The one with the two talents also came and said, 'Sir, you entrusted two talents to me. See, I have gained two more.' 23 His master answered, 'Well done, good and faithful slave! You have been faithful with a few things. I will put you in charge of many things. Enter into the joy of your master.' 24 Then the one who had received the one talent came and said, 'Sir, I knew that you were a hard man, harvesting where you did not sow, and gathering where you did not scatter seed, 25 so I was afraid, and I went and hid your talent in the ground. See, you have what is yours.' 26 But his master answered, 'Evil and lazy slave! So you knew that I harvest where I didn't sow and gather where I didn't scatter? 27 Then you should have deposited my money with the bankers, and on my return I would have received my money back with interest! 28 Therefore take the talent from him and give it to the one who has ten. 29 For the one who has will be given more, and he will have more than enough. But the one who does not have, even what he has will be taken from him. 30 And throw that worthless slave into the outer darkness, where there will be weeping and gnashing of teeth'" (Matthew 25:13-30).

Immaturity can be another decisive factor in why our gift is not working for us. This one may be a tough one for some to hear, accept or even relate to but at the end of the day it is the truth. Some of us have to grow up and mature into our gift. We and I say we, have languished in infancy in our spiritual development; still supping regularly on milk and bread when we need to mature into meat and potatoes. Until we reach a place where our gift can be exercised in its fullness, our gift won't work for us. We have to be mature for gift manifestation and then to handle the responsibility that is directly tied to our gift. Immaturity is a painful reality and a gift suppressor.

One of the hardest barriers to overcome, especially in our walk with Christ is unworthiness; feeling as though we are not worthy of the gifts God has given to us. More than that, ofttimes we feel unworthy of God's love and forgiveness. The word unworthy means undeserving, not a good risk, not deserving effort, lacking value or merit, or insufficient in worth. To feel unworthy is to feel that you are really worth-less... Worthless is defined as lacking value, valueless, useless, trashy, and paltry, having no good qualities, or deserving contempt. I intentionally put the hyphen between worth and less because I want you to take a minute and examine the separation. Of course the word is written worthless, but it bears consideration to look at the word in this way... worth-less. Upon closer examination, worth-less means less than in the comparison of worth to something or someone else. This clearly ties back to the barrier of intimidation and other barriers we have spoken about here. Insufficient... that is such a powerful connotation – feeling and emotion.

And that emotion is what so many of us battle with in our spiritual lives. We feel unworthy of God's grace and mercy. We feel valueless, trashy, and contemptible. We have condemned ourselves by our prior lifestyles, our previous sins. Even though we say we know God is a forgiving God, but we hold our sins and shame over our own heads. When we look in the proverbial mirror, what is reflected back to us is not the new creature God has created but that old man we refuse to let go of and let die. We don't see the newness of God's hand in our lives. Why is that? Because we feel insufficient, unworthy, worth-less.

I battled with feelings of unworthiness. I kept questioning myself and denying myself; telling myself that I couldn't do it or move forward in the use of my gift. I kept talking myself out of it. I kept making excuses not knowing exactly why I was making them. Then I was given clarity; painful clarity. The Lord said to me, "You keep making excuses because you don't think you are valuable enough. You really think you are worthless." That hit me like a ton of bricks. I had to think about what He said, and try to think about it through a clear lens. Then I realized, I kept looking into my past; looking at the things I didn't have, didn't do, didn't think I deserved. I felt unworthy. I didn't feel like I was worthy to have more than what I had. I felt worth-less. I am so grateful that God has never given me what I <u>deserve</u> because if He did...

The scripture says to 'love your neighbor as yourself'. But God said to me, the way you handle people is a reflection of the way you feel about yourself. He made me look at how I took care of my body, how I took care of my personal things. He gave me a natural look. He said the way you see things naturally is the way you feel about you on the inside. I said, 'Lord that's not good'. My house is junky, it's in disarray. There is nothing in order. And he said, that's the way you treat people, carelessly, frivolously. You think you are loving and caring with people but that is not the case. The gift I gave to you, you don't take care of. You don't because you don't feel like you are worthy or deserving of the gift. Until you can change your mind about you and the things I've given you, the gift will just sit there.

I was then reminded of one of my favorite scriptures: "We are god's children of the most high God. Now if I believe that to be true, that I am a god, then how could I feel so worth-less. If that's the case, then what do I really think about God? Is He worth-less? The only kind of gifts God gives is good gifts. He doesn't give bad gifts. The good gifts he gives are to those that are truly deserving of His goodness. Doesn't that really answer the question about our level of worth? If God didn't think us worthy, would he waste his time bestowing gifts upon us? Think about it. Breathing is a gift, walking, talking, thinking; these are all gifts. Put on top of that the spiritual gifts He so generously has given to us. Would He really do that if we were so worth-less? We have to get out of our own way to receive the gifts God has given to us. We are our greatest barrier to the gift. But if you are not in relationship with God personally then you gone miss this! (And I meant to say it just that way!)

The Spirit of the Lord spoke to me and said, deal with the Spirit of Fear. My people are struggling with this spirit and don't realize it because it has disguised itself as something else… concern or anxiety, worry, apprehension, alarm, trepidation—unease, nervousness or foreboding thoughts. We say things like: 'I'm not worried just concerned.'

According to the dictionary, fear is defined as dread, uneasiness, or anxiousness. But from a biblical standpoint, fear is more than a feeling, it is a spirit!

II Tim 1:7 says, "For God has not given us a spirit of fear and timidity, but of power, love, and self-discipline." NLT

Now it is time to set the record straight! Fear in no shape, form or fashion comes from God. I've heard people talk about God giving them a "healthy fear". I've heard others say that "some fear is good because it motivates you to make changes." Well guess what? If fear motivated you to make the change it will be the motivating factor to keep the change.

But who really wants to live in fear, where fear is the impetus for operation?

There are some of us who are using fear as a motivating factor right now. For example, there are a number of us who struggle with weight issues. At times, we are more conscientious of our weight than at other times. We diet, break the diet, make promises to keep the diet, become disenchanted with the diet, get frustrated with the diet, and the end result is still a struggle with our weight. Let's just suppose for a minute that we go to our physician for an examination and the issue of our weight comes up; it doesn't just come up, it dominates the doctor's conversation and he or she articulates a concern regarding our weight. "If you don't lose the weight, you will die a premature death!" To get a report like this from a doctor is frightening to say the least. Now of course, the delivery from the doctor would be much more sensitive and politically correct than I have said it here. But I don't want you to get caught up in comforting words and miss out on the message. If you don't lose the weight, you are going to die!

After we recover from the shock of the doctor's information, it is quite natural to be afraid for what could happen. So we go into overdrive to lose the weight because if we don't there are dire consequences. Now because of fear, we begin to take the diet much more seriously; not to suggest that we may not have been serious before, but now, there is a new and present focus... a premature and untimely death! Our dieting is driven by fear! We are diligent and dedicated and the weight begins to come off; the premature death is now not as imminent because we are addressing the problem. We are dealing with it because we can't live with the consequences of not dealing with it. The more weight we lose, the better we feel, the further the impending consequences are moved away from us. For some, it gets to a point where we are afraid to eat for fear of gaining the weight back that has been lost.

The question becomes, why was it necessary for fear to motivate you to take action, to move in a situation you already acknowledged needed to be addressed? Why was fear your motivator?

Another example of how we use fear as a 'motivator' is the fear of going without. This is especially true for those of us who may have grown up poor and had to go without the basic necessities. As a child, we may not have been able to control our circumstances and environments. Therefore as adults, we promise ourselves that we will never go without again, right? We will do whatever it takes to not be in that place again. Even if it means working 12 jobs, around the clock, we will do it because we are afraid of reverting back to a place of having nothing. We don't work nonstop because we like it! We forego spending quality time with friends and family because we have to work so we don't ever have to be without; not realizing or accepting that we are still living without because we don't have time to foster genuine relationships with family, friends... or God... We are motivated by the fear of not having. Again, is that really how we want to live? Do we need fear to motivate us to take the necessary action? To invest wisely so that we can have and not kill ourselves trying to make sure we have?

THE ANOINTING

When we are moved by the Holy Spirit we call it the ANOINTING. It empowers us; gets behind us and pushes us. The Holy Spirit gives us courage to be bold. It enables us to do things we could never do in our own strength. Feelings can't do this.

It is important to know that the presence of the spirit of

fear in your life brings with it an anointing as well; a negative destructive anointing. If you don't believe fear brings an anointing with it, ask the madman of Gadara. Possessed by a legion of demons, he had the strength of a hundred men, able to break chains and do superhuman feats. He had supernatural power, a satanic anointing, but still an anointing. This anointing made him miserable and wretched. Yes, fear makes you miserable!

I like to use definitions because then there is no question as to what is meant; the point is made clear. Miserable is defined as: (1) a miserable person, one who is profoundly unhappy or in great misfortune (2) a base, despicable, or vile person; (3) wretched.

Now, say this with me: Fear is bondage!

For a believer in Christ Jesus to live in bondage to fear is as unnatural as a fish trying to live out of water. Part of being born again is being born to freedom, being released from bondage of sin. And fear is sin because the Bible says that whatever is not of Faith is Sin (Rom 14:23). The apostle Paul also wrote:

Romans 8:11-15 (New Living Translation)

The Spirit of God, who raised Jesus from the dead, lives in you. And just as God raised Christ Jesus from the dead, he will give life to your mortal bodies by this same Spirit living within you.

Therefore, dear brothers and sisters, you have no obligation to do what your sinful nature urges you to do. For if you live by its dictates, you will die. But if through the power of the Spirit you put to death the deeds of your sinful nature, you will live. For all who are led by the Spirit of God are children of God.

So you have not received a spirit that makes you fearful slaves. Instead, you received God's Spirit when he adopted you as his own children. Now we call him, "Abba, Father."

Fear is totally alien, foreign to your re-born spirit. In fact, your spirit cannot produce fear. It has to come from the outside. You can receive fear, but you cannot manufacture it. You can act on it. You can be choked by it and let it paralyze you. Only you, by an act of your will, can keep this from happening!

Fear paralyzes you. It brings you to a condition of

helplessness, stoppage, inactivity, or inability to act. Listening to negative and fear based self talk from the enemy about you not being ready to be used by God because of your past or past failures is how fear becomes operationalized in your life. Instead of giving you wisdom, fear causes you to make poor decisions because of uncertainty and skepticism.

FIRST THINGS FIRST

Recognize when fear is trying to creep in. Fear sends his sidekick first to throw you off...his name is DOUBT— *hesitation, uncertainty, reservation, distrust, suspicious, skeptic, disbelieve.* Doubts job is to **prepare you** for the coming of fear; just like doubt got Adam and Eve in the Garden (Gen 3:9-10).

But the LORD God called to the man, "Where are you?" He answered, "I heard you in the garden, and I was afraid because I was naked; so I hid."

Why were they afraid, because:

- [] The devil wanted them and you to doubt God's promises
- [] The devil wanted them and you to doubt God's faithfulness
- [] The devil wanted them and you to doubt the power of the Word and the power in the name of God!

Don't forget: Doubt is the prep man for fear!

Some of you right now are listening to Mr. Doubt, the forerunner of fear, telling you:

- [] What you think is a gift really isn't a gift.

- [] Why would God entrust you with such a wonderfully powerful gift? Who are you?

- [] You don't deserve it!

Can I go a little deeper?

PRINCIPALS GOVERNING FEAR

There are two laws that every human being lives under, according to Romans 8:1-2; one is dominated by life and the other is dominated by death.

A law is defined as an established principle-confirmed-verified, validated, proven that it can be expected to function the same way every time. For example, the law of gravity says, what goes up must come down. It doesn't change. You speed you get a Ticket. You live and you die. It's a law. The law can be expected to function the same way every time.

Romans 8:1-2 (Amplified Bible)

Romans 8

1. THEREFORE, [there is] now no condemnation (no adjudging guilty of wrong) for those who are in Christ Jesus, who live [and] walk not after the dictates of the flesh, but after the dictates of the Spirit. (A)

2. For the law of the Spirit of life [which is] in Christ Jesus [the law of our new being] has freed me from the law of sin and of death.

Even as a Christian just because you are saved does not mean that you are living--active under the law of the Spirit of life. There is a part that you must play.

These two laws can be referred to as reciprocals of

each other. A reciprocal in mathematics is an expression or relationship so close to the other that they relate as one. Let's look at this example. Take the fraction 2/3 and turn it upside down to 3/2. If you look at this purely as a mathematical relationship, these two fractions are so close together that when multiplied by each other 2/3 x 3/2, they equal 1. This connotation can apply spiritually as well, especially if we are not careful. The enemy has been trying since his demise to make the word of God reciprocal. For every spiritual force and substance in the realm of life, there is a reciprocal force or substance in the realm of death.

- Life realm = hope
- Death realm= despair
- Life realm=agape love, the kind of love that gives and gives
- Death realm= total selfishness

Deuteronomy 30:19 (New Living Translation)

[19] *"Today I have given you the choice between life and death; between blessings and curses. Now I call on heaven and earth to witness the choice you make. Oh, that you would choose life, so that you and your descendants might live!*

So how do I deal with the Spirit of Fear? I'm Glad you asked.

LET THE WORD DO THE WORK

This leads me to the next reason why people feel their gift is not working for them… faith, or more specifically, a lack thereof. One of the most powerful forces in the realm of the law of life is what? FAITH!

Here is a test to see if you were following along. Are you ready?

What is the reciprocal of Faith? Fear, that's right.

Next question: How does one gain Faith? That's right from hearing the Word of God; not just hearing the preacher, bishop, minister or the elders preach to you but Hearing it come out of your own mouth. You see if you are talking you can't entertain thoughts at the same time. ***Speak the word to shut down the thoughts***. You wanna know why some of you are being whipped by fear, and attacked by his co-conspirator, doubt? Because you're not saying anything that will move heaven on your behalf.

Too often we respond to fear and are motivated by fear because the route fear suggests seems the easier of the two.

Faith and operating in faith is hard work. However, easy is not always best.

John 16:33 (New Living Translation)

³³ I have told you all this so that you may have peace in me. Here on earth you will have many trials and sorrows. But take heart, because I have overcome the world."

If we truly have faith in God and as a result, faith in the gifts God has given us, then we understand the importance of operating in that faith according to His instruction. In other words, it's His way or no way and when you decide to do it your way here is what the Word of the Lord says about that:

1 Peter 2:7-11   *⁷ Yes, you who trust him recognize the honor God has given him. But for those who reject him,* (Because of your concern)

"The stone that the builders rejected has now become the cornerstone." ⁸ And,   "He is the stone that makes people stumble, the rock that makes them fall." They stumble because they do not obey God's word, and so they meet the fate that was planned for them.

As long as the enemy can creep in with doubts and fear absent faith, he has you every time. The magnificent thing about God and His favor, however, is that doubt and fear does not have to be victorious. He reminds us in the scripture of why He saw fit to give us the specific gifts he has.

[9] *But you are not like that, for you are a chosen people. You are royal priests, a holy nation, and God's very own possession. As a result, you can show others the goodness of God, for he called you out of the darkness (Fear, anxiety, worry, hopelessness, and uncertainty) into his wonderful light.*

[10] *"Once you had no identity as a people; now you are God's people. Once you received no mercy; now you have received God's mercy."*

When we know without a shadow of a doubt who and whose we are, then fear cannot abide!

"We were put on this earth to achieve our greatest self, to live out our purpose, and to do it fearlessly" (Steve Maraboli, "Life the Truth and Being Free).

UPROOTING THE SPIRIT OF FEAR

Isaiah 41:10 (Amplified Bible)

[10]Fear not [there is nothing to fear], for I am with you; do not look around you in terror and be dismayed, for I am your God. I will strengthen and harden you to difficulties, yes, I will help you; yes, I will hold you up and retain you with My [victorious] right hand of rightness and justice.

Four Keys to Uprooting the Spirit of Fear

Below are proven ways that will uproot, disengage and disentangle the spirit of fear.

The first is to Make a Quality Decision:

In order to be free you have to make a decision to be free. It sounds simple but this is the hardest part to do. The Lord told me years ago that when I begin to hate the sin that I was in like He hates it, then and only then will I become free from bondage. Some of you like mess....you like drama...and you like draining the saints because you need some attention, but the devil is a liar. It stops here today. I declare that you are on the road to recover all. You got over in this realm by an act of your will whether you realize it or not and it is going to take an act of your will to get back. You must choose faith over fear if you want to be free.

Secondly, understand the magnitude of Gods Protection:

Isaiah 43:1-2 (New Living Translation) says, "But now, O Jacob, listen to the Lord who created you. O Israel, the one who formed you says, "Do not be afraid, for I have ransomed you. I have called you by name; you are mine. When you go through deep waters, I will be with you. When you go through rivers of difficulty, you will not drown. When you walk through the fire of oppression, you will not be burned up; the flames will not consume you."

When we understand how big God really is and how much He loves us and has invested in us, there is no reason to be afraid or to operate in a fearful way. God has already promised us protection. What is there to fear?

Thirdly, Develop Confidence in God's Promises:

Keep in mind the number one strategy of the enemy is to get you to entertain doubt about the promises of God. Remember that spirit is the forerunner to opening the door of fear. Well how do I shut the door when doubt comes? You shut it by FAITH and faith comes by HEARING and HEARING by the Word of God.

And lastly, Employ Love:

1 John 4:17-18 (New Living Translation)

17 And as we live in God, our love grows more perfect. So we will not be afraid on the Day of Judgment, but we can face him with confidence because we live like Jesus here in this world.

18 Such love has no fear, because perfect love expels all fear. If we are afraid, it is for fear of punishment, and this shows that we have not fully experienced his perfect love.

If there is fear there is something in your life in the area of Love that needs to be examined. The word Love in the Greek is agape meaning the kind of love that gives without expecting anything in return. How do you display this kind of love....Obedience to Gods' word? Obedience is the only standard of measure of your love for God. It is not based on how you feel but what you do...1John 5:3 says "For this is the love of God, that we keep his commandments: and his commandments are not grievous. See when you obey God it causes you to do the very thing Satan fears you will do—things like:

- ☐ Spend time with God

- ☐ Study the Word

- ☐ Learn the Word

The reason why some of you are not successful in the things of God is because you won't come to church. Your disobedience to your Shepard's puts you in harms way. They have designed a way for you to be successful in your walk with Christ through all the educational courses and mid week services and you won't come to any because your life is full of yourself. Yes I said it. You're to full of you. You know I'm right. But you wanna drain the saints when you go through… had you had your end in one of these seats when the doors opened you'd get your deliverance, you'd get your instructions for the battle but no, you choose to live under the second law…this only applies to the guilty….say amen and you won't look guilty. The Devil has intimidated me and my brother and sisters too long and now I'm coming out fighting.

THREE THINGS TO KEEP YOU FREE FROM FEAR

1. Live right—plain and simple

2. Speak the Word—we are going to repent and declare the word over our lives today

3. Stay in the light of His Presence—when you screw up don't hide like Adam and Eve, be like David and repent and get cleansed so you can move forward.

We are all human, and in our humanness, we are imperfect. There will be times when we are afraid, when we let fear get the better of us. Fear locks our gifts in place and stifles our growth. In those times, there are declarations you can make that will dispel your fearful feelings, thoughts and ideas:

Hebrews 4:16 (Amplified Bible)

16Let us then fearlessly and confidently and boldly draw near to the throne of grace (the throne of God's unmerited favor to us sinners), that we may receive mercy [for our failures] and find grace to help in good time for every need [appropriate help and well-timed help, coming just when we need it]. Amen

Scripture Declarations for Dealing with Fear

Psalm 23:4 (Amplified Bible)

Yes, though I walk through the [deep, sunless] valley of the shadow of death, I will fear or dread no evil, for You are with me; Your rod [to protect] and Your staff [to guide], they comfort me.

Psalm 27:1 (Amplified Bible)

[1]THE LORD is my Light and my Salvation--whom shall I fear or dread? The Lord is the Refuge and Stronghold of my life--of whom shall I be afraid?

Although there may be other factors that have been employed causing us to question why our gift is not working for us, the last one I will deal with is the loss of hope. Just as with the other factors that impede our gifts, losing hope can be devastating and place our gifts into a solitary and stagnant place. But what is hope? That word is often thrown around so cavalierly with little regard for its truest meaning. Hope is the feeling that what you truly desire can be had. It's a feeling of great expectation knowing that the object or objects of your truest desire are possible.

When all hope has been lost, there are no expectations; no desires; no possibilities… not even wishful thinking. Living without hope takes the purpose and promise out of life. A gift cannot work or be manifested in a hope-less environment. But once again, God has already promised us that He would abide with us even when we truly feel that there is no hope. One of my favorite biblical stories of hope is that of Abraham and Sarah. God had made a promise to Abraham and Sarah that they would have a child. Their faith was truly tested as God's promise was not immediately fulfilled. Because of their advanced ages, they felt that all hope was lost, that they would never have the child Sarah so desperately wanted. But Abraham and Sarah remained true to the promises of God, and as they say, the rest was history.

"And without becoming weak in faith he contemplated his own body, now as good as dead since he was about a hundred years old, and the deadness of Sarah's womb; yet, with respect to the promise of God, he did not waver in unbelief, but grew strong in faith, giving glory to God, and being fully assured that what He had promised, He was able also to perform" (Rom. 4:19-21).

Of Sarah, the writer to the Hebrews declared, "By faith even Sarah herself received ability to conceive, even beyond the proper time of life, since she considered Him faithful who had promised" (Heb. 11:11). Their faith was rewarded; Sarah had a son and they called his name Isaac, which means "laughter." And Sarah told us why they gave him that name: "God has made laughter for me; everyone who hears will laugh with me" (Gen. 21:6). Her laugh of doubt had turned to a laugh of triumphant joy.

The joy of the birth of their long awaited child is certainly something to celebrate. But let's not overlook the greater message in this story. When Abraham and Sarah felt like all hope was lost, God delivered on the promise He had made to them. It may not have been in the time that they would have preferred but God's timing is perfected. Had he delivered the child to them earlier, there is a possibility that their faithfulness to God may have waivered. If God can deliver on a promise to Abraham who was nearly 100 years of age and Sarah who was 90, certainly He can and will deliver on the promise He has made to you. Your giftedness is God's promise. There is no reason to lose hope in this situation. If you stay in the will of God and nurture your gift, I promise you God will deliver!

Consider this: your gift may be incubating even now. Whether your inhibitor is mental, physical, psychological, spiritual, fear based, or immaturity, your gift is waiting to be unleashed!

Points to Consider...

- Why do you feel your gift is not working for you?

- Are there other barriers not mentioned that you struggle with?

- What are your personal struggles regarding your gift?

- What has been holding your gift back from full operationalization?

- Have you faced some new realities now that you have confronted your gift inhibitors?

_____

_____

_____

_____

_____

_____

_____

_____

_____

_____

_____

_____

_____

_____

_____

_____

_____

_____

_____

_____

_____

_____

_____

_____

_____

_____

_____

_____

_____

_____

The Choice is Yours

In the preceding pages, we have defined what a gift is. We have also talked about the many barriers to your gift and why your gift may not be working for you. Now, the list of barriers is not by any means an exhaustive list. There may be other barriers, blockades, and inhibitors you are dealing with that may have not been discussed. That doesn't mean you don't have to determine what the barriers to the release of your gift are in order for you to move forward.

The Choice is Yours! Sounds simple enough, right? We all have choices, and we make innumerable choices every day. Some of the choices we make tend to be on automatic pilot, we really don't give them too much thought, like brushing our teeth, eating, driving, or combing our hair. (I don't personally have the hair combing issue, but you get my point!) However, with other choices, we tend to labor over them; finding it difficult to decide just what is the best choice for us. We may pray about it, consult friends about it, and even stress and worry about. These are the kinds of choices that are deliberate, prayerfully well thought out and intentioned.

Either way, choosing can be very difficult, but it has to be done.

A choice is a two step process. First, there is the mental decision as to what you will do. Your cognition is operationalized to weigh the pros and cons, to consider, to pray or to mediate to make the conscientious choice. I have to laugh when I think about some of the choices I have made in my own life; whether I really gave them enough thought or did I act without thinking. That's why it's important to fully understand that a choice is a two step process, not just one. Our minds have to be engaged in order to affect a choice. If we allow ourselves the opportunity to think and consider, then choices are not made hastily but deliberately. Haste can often lead to poor decision making. At the same time, a choice is necessary. Too many of us have languished in the land of indecision; causing our gifts to languish with us. There is a balance between haste, rushing and inactivity but indecision is not a choice.

For many of us, deciding to put our gift into full operation is that second kind of choice; the kind we struggle with, are concerned about, consult God and others we trust about. When I think about making choices, one of the biblical stories that come to mind is that of the four lepers.

"Four men were before the gate as lepers," separated from human society, according to the law in. These men being on the point of starvation, resolved to invade the camp of the Syrians, and carried out this resolution in the evening twilight, not the morning twilight on account of 2 Kings 7:12, where the king is said to have received the news of the flight of the Syrians during the night. Coming to "the end of the Syrian camp," i.e., to the outskirts of it on the city side, they found no one there. For (2 Kings 7:6, 2 Kings 7:7) "the Lord had caused the army of the Syrians to hear a noise of chariots and horses, a noise of a great army," so that, believing the king of Israel to have hired the kings of the Hittites and Egyptians to fall upon them, they fled from the camp in the twilight with regard to their life. The miracle, by which God delivered Samaria from the famine or from surrendering to the foe, consisted in an oral delusion, namely, in the fact that the besiegers thought they heard the march of hostile armies from the north and south, and were seized with such panic terror that they fled in the greatest haste, leaving behind them their baggage, and their beasts of draught and burden. It is impossible to decide

whether the noise which they heard had any objective reality, say a miraculous buzzing in the air, or whether it was merely a deception of the senses produced in their ears by God; and this is a matter of no importance, since in either case it was produced miraculously by God (**bible**.cc/2_kings/7-3.htm).

These men had a very difficult choice to make; go back to the city where they would surely die, or go towards the enemy where death was certainly imminent. But the basic, natural need for food caused them to make a decision; regardless of the risk. The enemy had food. They knew that. The four lepers made the decision to satisfy their immediate hunger and go towards the food. God, in his awesome power, intervened on their behalf and called the enemy to kill himself, leaving the food for the lepers to eat.

What is the point of this story? There's one thing to make the mental decision or the choice to do something but there is no manifestation without movement! These men had to get up and go in the direction of the enemy in order to execute their choice! They couldn't sit still, having made the choice and wait for the resolution they desired. They had to physically get up and move!

Of the many gifts the Almighty has given us is the ability to move. We have the activity of our limbs that execute the choices we make in our minds. Faith without works is dead. A gift without movement is a dead gift.

When researching for this book, I ran across a concept that is all too familiar to many of us. Nike's motto is 'Just do it', right? We know how popular of a company Nike is and how many millions upon millions of dollars the company has made. But in my research, I ran across the true meaning of the Nike swoosh, you know the logo that is on all of their accessories. The swoosh really represents a wing. The Nike logo is based from ancient history and the statue Winged Victory. Winged Victory of Somathrace is also referred to as the Nike of Somathrace. It is a statue from the 2nd century B.C. What is interesting about this statue is the figure has no head, and no arms. You get the sense that the statue has legs, but they are partially hidden in the fabric of her clothing. What struck me about this statue is that in the absence of having the 'activity of her limbs' she still has movement. The idea? She has no head, so there is no ability to think. She doesn't have arms or legs, so technically she cannot move. But in the absence of what we feel is required for movement, she has wings which means she can fly. God gave her wings, so she can just do it. It may not be easy, but she can move, she can fly.

What excuse do we have to move? We are clothed in our right mind. If you are reading this, then you have the desire somewhere deep inside to let the gift you have been blessed with out. You obviously have cognition; the mind is working and active. We have the activity of our limbs. Prayerfully our physical movement is not inhibited, nor the mental movement necessary to actualize movement. We have everything we need to move. Remember, the choice to move is yours! Is there something still holding you back?

Deuteronomy 30:19 says, *"Today I have given you the choice between life and death, between blessings and curses. Now I call on heaven and earth to witness the choice you make. Oh, that you would choose life, so that you and your descendants might live!*

One thing we cannot forget is that there is an assignment attached to your gift. An assignment is a task or post of duty that must be completed, given to us by one we hold in high regard. Think about it. Would you be willing to execute an assignment from someone you don't respect, trust, or value? Probably not... In order for you to seriously consider executing the assignment, you must first respect the person the assignment comes from. Now, some of us may think we make our own assignments. In some cases that may be true. But I would like to think when we are talking about gifts from God, then the assignment attached to the gift emanates from Him. If you know that, then maybe that's why making the choice to move is so difficult. You don't want to disappoint Him; you may be fearful you don't have what it takes to complete the assignment. Maybe you are scared to fail or you feel the attached assignment is too big. I know I have certainly felt that way on more than one occasion. One thing we can't forget, God won't put on us more than we can bear! That doesn't just apply to burdens or tests and trials. It also applies to the gifts we have been given.

Although making the choice is hard, when You make the choice, God makes the provision! That's right, He makes the provision. We have to remember, even before our birth, even before the foundations of man were poured,

God knew exactly what your gifts would be, what your assignment was and what provisions would be necessary for you to successfully operate in your giftedness. When you think about it, the choice should become easier not harder when you know God's got your back from the beginning.

Although I indicated earlier making a choice is a two step process, there is something that goes hand in hand with that I think it is important for us to be reminded of. Again, this may well tie in for you and me into one of the barriers of unleashing our gift. We are what we think. I know you have heard many a saying and old adage about this very thing, but it is so true. We really are what we think. After cognition is operationalized, and even if we have the full capacity of our limbs for movement and mobility, what we think and subsequently speak out of our mouths can either help or hinder the choice process. We govern our lives by our thoughts and mouths. When you speak negativity, it is truly a reflection of the negative thoughts in your head. The same holds true when you speak positivity over yourself and over your life.

Romans 12: 6-8 says, *"We have different gifts, according to the grace given to each of us. If your gift is prophesying, then prophesy in accordance with your faith; [7] if it is serving, then serve; if it is teaching, then teach; [8] if it is to encourage, then give encouragement; if it is giving, then give generously; if it is to lead, do it diligently; if it is to show mercy, do it cheerfully."*

Don't negate the power of God's gifting to you by negative self talk. "Life and death lies in the power of the tongue." Speak life. Make your tongue work on your behalf. We all know the tongue is as powerful as a two edge sword. Use it to cut in favor of you and your gift and not cut against the grain of the powerhouse of gifts God has placed upon you. Speak life over yourself and over your gifts.

Remember, whatsoever you speak you will have. *"Therefore I tell you, whatever you ask for in prayer, believe that you have received it, and it will be yours" (Matthew 11:24).*

Joshua 24:15 says, *As far as me and my house, we will serve the Lord."* When you speak with conviction like Joshua did that is a definitive choice. A part of our service to God is making our gifts work. To serve is to help or do for someone; to act on behalf of someone else. We have already made the conscientious choice to serve God. That's evident. But part of our service to Him is using the gifts God gave us for His glory and edification. Our service to God is incomplete if we are sitting on our gifts, being lazy with our gifts or not making the choice to use our gifts.

Once we have made the choice to use our Gifts, God will anoint the gifts He activates. Isn't that a blessing! To know once we decide to use what we have been given God will add another level of anointing to our lives and make the gift work in ways we never thought possible. You see, we all have an idea of what our gift would look like if we put it into motion. Whatever the divine gift, we have given some consideration as to how our gift would manifest itself and how powerful the gift would be. But whatever you imagine; whatever you see as your gift being magnified at its highest level, God has a level of anointing he will unleash on top of that. Now, imagine the power of the gift!

Lastly, faith is expectation. To have faith means to live in expectancy. Faith moves you towards your goal and your gift is a part of that movement. I have to go back to an old standby; one of my favorite scriptures. *"Now faith is the substance of things hoped for, the evidence of things not seen"*

(Hebrews 11:1). The scripture says Now faith... It doesn't say, faith for the future, past tense faith or later faith. It says clearly NOW faith! That means right now, at this appointed time, in this moment faith.

Now is the time to know what your gift is. Now is the time to understand why your gift has not been working for you. Now is the time to understand what those barriers are that are blocking your gift from becoming operational and being used for God's glory. Now is the time to render fear, laziness, jealousy, unworthiness, self doubt and hopelessness, powerless over your gift. Now is the time to take what is rightfully yours, given to you by the Most High God, the Creator of Heaven and Earth and the benefactor of everything He's created. Now is the time to make the choice to move! Now is the time to live in expectancy, knowing God has given you everything you need. Now is the time to have right now Faith! Now is the time to **Unleash Your Gift!**

About the Author

Elder Donald B. Douglas a native of East St. Louis, Il, has been in the music industry well over 30 years. His music career has allowed him the opportunity to teach award winning Jr. high and high school choirs, travel with nationally acclaimed production companies, perform at the Muny Theater, travel with renowned jazz artist, open for some of the key gospel groups in the nation today, and many others too numerous to list.

Elder Douglas has been married to his suitable mate and partner in ministry Rachelle R. Douglas for six years. They have three beautiful children, Kenyjah, Marvin and Marie all whom he cherishes dearly.

His music ministry has taken him across this country singing the gospel before thousands of people. There is a healing anointing that is ushered in through this man's ministry gift of song. His love and devotion to Christ is evident in his ministering of music to God's people.

Elder Douglas was educated in the parochial school district and a graduate of Lindenwood University with a degree in Human Resource Management has been a member of Power of Change Christian Church since December of 2000. Elder Douglas has been in ministry close to 20 yrs. He serves as the Administrative Elder over Membership, Assimilations Director as well as the interim Minister of Music and a teacher in the Education Department of POCCC. Elder Douglas believes that his life is not his own but everything that God has deposited in him belongs to those he serves. Seeing God's people set free from the yoke of the enemy is his driving force.

Elder Douglas has travel across this country ministering in song and the word. Elder Douglas also has his own personal ministry; <u>Sounds of Unlimited Love</u> where he trains those called to the music ministry whether it is leaders of worship, Ministers of Music training or vocal training. Elder Douglas says that if he had a theme song that describes him best it would be "I Give Myself Away So You Can Use Me."

Unbeknownst to Elder Douglas, his gifts would be called to action once again, but in a very different way. He would be called to use his gifts in the execution of his new book, "Unleashing the Gift". Although it had been prophesied to Elder Douglas many years ago he would write a book, the prophesy was tucked away, and his focus remained on his music. But God's calling would not be denied and Elder Douglas was obedient in answering that divine call. Elder Douglas has many new writing projects in store and is excited about the prospects. He appreciates all those who have prayed for him and supported him with "Unleashing to Gift", and looks forward to continue in bringing forth the power of God through the written word.

CPSIA information can be obtained at www.ICGtesting.com
Printed in the USA
LVOW12s2043280713

345008LV00001B/10/P